SWEDISH
CHRISTMAS TREATS

SWEDISH
CHRISTMAS TREATS

60 Recipes for Delicious
Holiday Snacks and Desserts

Chocolates, Cakes, Truffles, Fudge,
and Other Amazing Sweets

Lena Söderström

Photography by Eva Hildén

Racehorse
Publishing

Visit our website at www.skyhorsepublishing.com.

10 9 8 7 6 5 4 3 2 1

Library of Congress Cataloging-in-Publication Data is available on file.

Text, recipes, and styling by Lena Söderström
Photography by Eva Hildén
Photo of author by Camilla Lindqvist
Design by Monica Sundberg
Edited by Mattias Pettersson
Repro by Italgraf Media
Cover repro by TBP

ISBN: 978-1-63158-383-4
eISBN: 978-1-5107-7415-5

Printed in China

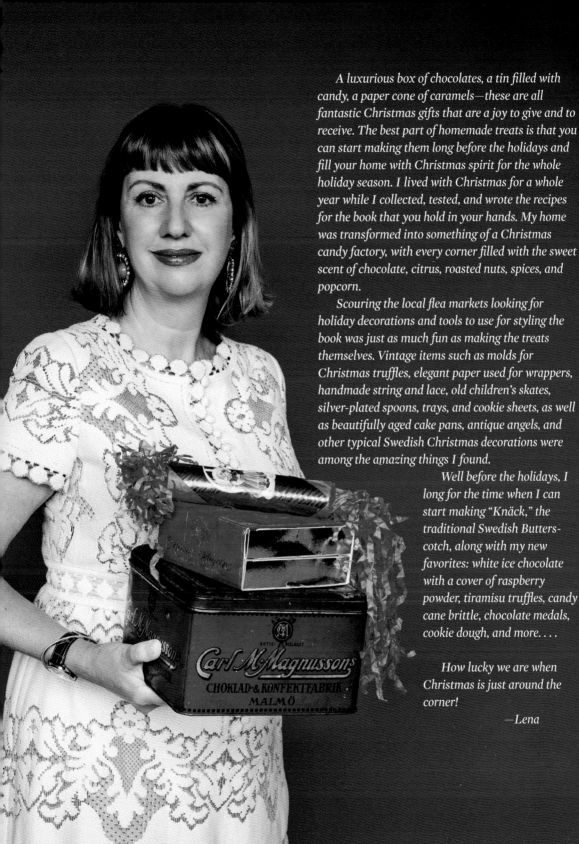

A luxurious box of chocolates, a tin filled with candy, a paper cone of caramels—these are all fantastic Christmas gifts that are a joy to give and to receive. The best part of homemade treats is that you can start making them long before the holidays and fill your home with Christmas spirit for the whole holiday season. I lived with Christmas for a whole year while I collected, tested, and wrote the recipes for the book that you hold in your hands. My home was transformed into something of a Christmas candy factory, with every corner filled with the sweet scent of chocolate, citrus, roasted nuts, spices, and popcorn.

Scouring the local flea markets looking for holiday decorations and tools to use for styling the book was just as much fun as making the treats themselves. Vintage items such as molds for Christmas truffles, elegant paper used for wrappers, handmade string and lace, old children's skates, silver-plated spoons, trays, and cookie sheets, as well as beautifully aged cake pans, antique angels, and other typical Swedish Christmas decorations were among the amazing things I found.

Well before the holidays, I long for the time when I can start making "Knäck," the traditional Swedish Butters-cotch, along with my new favorites: white ice chocolate with a cover of raspberry powder, tiramisu truffles, candy cane brittle, chocolate medals, cookie dough, and more. . . .

How lucky we are when Christmas is just around the corner!

—Lena

CHOCOLATE CANDY CANE BRITTLE

INGREDIENTS

1 TBSP VEGETABLE OIL
1¼ CUPS GRANULATED SUGAR
3.5 OZ MILK OR DARK CHOCOLATE (55–70%)
4 TBSP CRUSHED CANDY CANES

Cover a cookie sheet with parchment paper and brush it with the oil. In a deep saucepan (approximately 8 inches in diameter), melt the sugar over medium heat while stirring. Increase the heat when the sugar starts to caramelize and is light brown in color, and quickly turn out the liquid sugar onto the parchment paper. Use a spatula to spread it out evenly and leave it to cool and set.

Melt the chocolate (see instructions on page 16), pour it over the brittle, and spread it out evenly. Garnish with the crushed candy canes while it's still warm and let it cool and set. Break it into smaller pieces or crush the brittle when it's ready.

TIPS AND TRICKS

Give this chocolate brittle as a gift or keep it for yourself. It's easy to make, delicious to eat, and it looks very "Christmassy"!

WHITE "ICE" CHOCOLATE

with a raspberry blanket

YIELDS 24 PIECES

INGREDIENTS

10.5 OZ WHITE CHOCOLATE
⅓ CUP + 1 TBSP HEAVY CREAM
CUP (1.75 OZ) SOLID COCONUT OIL
RASPBERRY POWDER

Chop the white chocolate into small pieces. In a small saucepan, heat the cream with the coconut oil until the oil has completely melted. Take the pan off the heat and add the chocolate while stirring until it's melted, and the mixture is smooth. Pour the chocolate mixture onto a 6 x 8-inch cookie sheet or tray covered with parchment paper. Place the cookie sheet/tray in a cool place to set for 2 to 3 hours or overnight. When the chocolate is set, use a sieve to sprinkle with the raspberry powder and cut it into squares. Store in a cool place.

TIPS AND TRICKS

This so-called "Ice" chocolate is covered in a delicious blanket of pink raspberry powder. Buy the powder online or in a specialty store or make your own powder. The recipe for your own powder can be found on page 104.

CASHEW BRITTLE

INGREDIENTS

⅓ CUP + 1 TBSP CASHEW
NUTS, SALTED OR UNSALTED

1 TBSP VEGETABLE OIL

1¼ CUPS GRANULATED SUGAR

Chop the nuts coarsely. Cover a cookie sheet with parchment paper and brush the paper with the oil. In a small but deep saucepan (about 8 inches in diameter), gently melt the sugar on medium heat while stirring. Increase the heat when the sugar starts to caramelize and is light brown in color, and quickly turn out the liquid sugar onto the parchment paper. Use a spatula to spread it out evenly, and sprinkle with the nuts. Let it cool and set. When the brittle has set and is hard, break it, or crush it into bite-size pieces.

TIPS AND TRICKS

Eat the brittle like candy or chop it into smaller pieces with a pestle and mortar to be used for dessert toppings (see Christmas Parfait recipe on page 50). The brittle is just as delicious with salted or unsalted nuts.

CHOCOLATE-DIPPED "KOLA" CARAMELS

with flaky sea salt

MAKES 25 PIECES

INGREDIENTS

1¼ CUPS HEAVY CREAM
1¼ CUPS GRANULATED SUGAR
⅓ CUP + 1 TBSP GOLDEN SYRUP
1 TBSP BUTTER
1 TBSP VEGETABLE OIL
FOR BRUSHING
7 OZ DARK CHOCOLATE (55–70%)
FLAKY SEA SALT
CANDY/FOOD THERMOMETER

In a heavy pan, combine cream, sugar, and syrup, and heat while stirring. Use a candy/food thermometer to check the temperature of the mixture and continue heating without a lid until the temperature reaches 248–257°F (or 120–125°C). Keep stirring the mixture from time to time.

Remove the pan from the heat and add the butter while stirring.

Pour the mixture onto a tray or cookie sheet (about 6 x 8 inches in size), which has been covered with parchment paper brushed with the oil. Before the mixture cools down completely, use a knife or scissors to cut it into pieces. Leave the caramel pieces to cool and set completely.

Melt the chocolate (see page 16) and let it cool but not set. Dip the caramels in the chocolate and place them on parchment paper. Sprinkle the caramels with the flaky sea salt and let them cool. Store the caramels in a tin with a lid.

TIPS AND TRICKS

For those who love licorice, add 2 tablespoons licorice powder or 3 tablespoons finely crushed "Turkish Pepper candy" to the caramel mixture and whisk until it's smooth. Then follow the instructions above. You can find these online or in a specialty store.

CHOCOLATE MELTING TUTORIAL

The easy way to melt chocolate:

In this book, you'll find many recipes that include chocolate, and often involve melting the chocolate.

- The best way to melt chocolate is to use a double boiler or a "Bain-Marie," but if you don't have one, you can create your own by using two pans or one pan and a bowl (see image on next page).
- Chocolate can also be melted in a microwave oven in accordance with instructions on the chocolate wrapper, online, or in your microwave oven user manual, but make sure that you don't burn the chocolate.

DOUBLE-BOILING OR USING YOUR OWN "BAIN-MARIE":

- Boil water in a small pan (approximately 6 inches in diameter) or in the bottom part of a double boiler, if you have one.
- Chop or break the chocolate into equal size pieces and place them in the top part of a double boiler or in a deep bowl or pan that can withstand heat that is larger than the pan that you're using to boil the water.
- Take the pan off the heat and place the dish with the chocolate pieces on top of the water pan or in the top part of your double boiler. Stir until all the pieces have melted.
- Alternatively, you can start by melting 2/3 of the chocolate pieces. Once the chocolate has melted, then add the rest of the chocolate and let it melt while stirring continuously with a balloon whisk. This way the melted chocolate will be at a lower temperature and the consistency will be slightly thicker. This works really well if you're planning to use the chocolate for dipping candy in chocolate.

TIPS AND TRICKS

Make sure not to add any water to the chocolate during the melting process. If this happens the chocolate becomes grainy. Always store chocolate well-wrapped and in a dry and cool place.

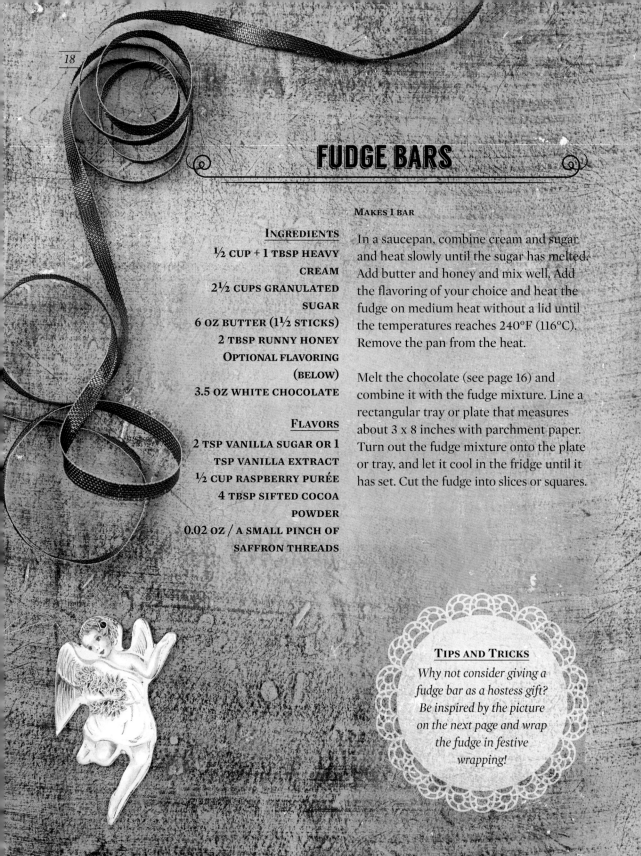

FUDGE BARS

MAKES 1 BAR

INGREDIENTS

½ CUP + 1 TBSP HEAVY
CREAM
2½ CUPS GRANULATED
SUGAR
6 OZ BUTTER (1½ STICKS)
2 TBSP RUNNY HONEY
OPTIONAL FLAVORING
(BELOW)
3.5 OZ WHITE CHOCOLATE

FLAVORS

2 TSP VANILLA SUGAR OR 1
TSP VANILLA EXTRACT
½ CUP RASPBERRY PURÉE
4 TBSP SIFTED COCOA
POWDER
0.02 OZ / A SMALL PINCH OF
SAFFRON THREADS

In a saucepan, combine cream and sugar and heat slowly until the sugar has melted. Add butter and honey and mix well. Add the flavoring of your choice and heat the fudge on medium heat without a lid until the temperatures reaches 240°F (116°C). Remove the pan from the heat.

Melt the chocolate (see page 16) and combine it with the fudge mixture. Line a rectangular tray or plate that measures about 3 x 8 inches with parchment paper. Turn out the fudge mixture onto the plate or tray, and let it cool in the fridge until it has set. Cut the fudge into slices or squares.

TIPS AND TRICKS

Why not consider giving a fudge bar as a hostess gift? Be inspired by the picture on the next page and wrap the fudge in festive wrapping!

BANANA CHIPS AND HONEY TRUFFLES

Makes 20 truffles

INGREDIENTS
7 OZ DARK CHOCOLATE
1⅔ CUPS BANANA CHIPS
⅓ CUP + 1 TSP HEAVY CREAM
1 TBSP LIQUID HONEY
1 TBSP BUTTER

Chop the chocolate into pieces with a knife and crush the banana chips in a mixer. In a small pan (about 9 inches in diameter), combine the cream and honey and bring to boil. Take the pan off the heat, add the chocolate, and let it melt while stirring with a whisk until the truffle mixture is smooth. Add the butter while whisking, and 3 tablespoons of the banana chips.

Turn out the mixture onto a tray or cookie sheet (about 6 x 8 inches) and let it cool. Cover with plastic wrap and place in the fridge to cool for 2 to 4 hours or until the mixture can be shaped into balls. When you've shaped the truffles into balls, roll them in the rest of the crushed banana chips, making sure that you press the mixture into the chips so that they stick to the truffles.

TIPS AND TRICKS

Give a box of truffles as a gift. Make one of more types of truffles. For example, you can make White Chocolate Truffles according to the recipe on page 78 and garnish them with chopped almonds. You could also add some Snowballs (see recipe on page 93).

CHOCOLATE SILVER SPOONS

Makes 6 to 8 spoons

Ingredients

6–8 nice vintage spoons
3.5 oz white chocolate
3.5 oz dark chocolate
(55–70%)
Edible sprinkles
(silver and stars)

Place the spoons so that they are supported and easy to fill, for example in a deep box. Melt both chocolates separately (see page 16) and divide between the spoons. Garnish with some sprinkles and let the spoons cool. Keep them in the fridge until you're ready to serve them.

Tips and Tricks

It can't be any easier than this! Look for vintage silver spoons at flea markets or in antique and vintage stores. Use larger spoons for adults and teaspoons for kids. You can enjoy the spoons like a chocolate lollipop, or you can make a lovely chocolate drink by sticking a spoon in a cup of warm milk and letting the chocolate melt.

FRENCH SOFT NOUGAT

MAKES 12 TO 15 PIECES

INGREDIENTS

1¼ CUPS GOLDEN OR WHITE EXTRA
LIGHT SUGAR SYRUP
⅓ CUP + 1 TBSP RUNNY HONEY
⅓ CUP + 1 TBSP LIQUID GLUCOSE
2 EGG WHITES AT ROOM TEMPERATURE
3 TBSP GRANULATED SUGAR
7 OZ TOASTED HAZELNUTS
(COARSELY CHOPPED)
3.5 OZ PEELED PISTACHIOS
⅓ CUP + 1 TBSP DRIED CRANBERRIES
OR CHERRIES (WITHOUT PITS)
POWDERED SUGAR FOR SPRINKLING
CANDY/FOOD THERMOMETER

TIPS AND TRICKS

This is the kind of candy that will appeal to those who don't mind some extra work. The homemade nougat is delicious and much better than store-bought options, and it's also a lot less expensive! If you need to serve many people you can cut the strips into thinner pieces.

In a heavy pan, combine the syrup, honey, and glucose while stirring. Bring to medium heat. Use your thermometer to make sure that the temperature reaches 257°F (125°C), but not higher, before you take the pan off the heat.

With an electric mixer, beat the egg whites until they hold stiff peaks. Add the sugar, little by little, while beating the meringue mixture until it has a smooth and shiny consistency. Add the honey, syrup, and glucose mixture to the meringue mixture and beat until it's smooth, for about 5 minutes. Add the hazelnuts, pistachios, and cranberries (or cherries).

On a large cutting board covered with a double sheet of parchment paper, sift the powdered sugar and spread the nougat mixture on top. Sift powdered sugar over the nougat and cover it with another double sheet of parchment paper. Press with your hands on the paper to shape the mixture to about ¾-inch thickness. Let it rest for at least three hours, but preferably overnight. When the nougat has set, cut it into long strips with a sharp kitchen knife.

GOLD DUST-COVERED DARK CHOCOLATE TRUFFLES

MAKES ABOUT 20 TRUFFLES

INGREDIENTS

9 OZ DARK CHOCOLATE (55–70%)
⅓ CUP + 1 TBSP HEAVY CREAM
3 TBSP MUSCOVADO BROWN SUGAR (LIGHT OR DARK)
1¾ OZ BUTTER AT ROOM TEMPERATURE (JUST UNDER ½ STICK OF BUTTER)
2–3 TBSP COGNAC OR RUM

TO GARNISH:

7 OZ DARK CHOCOLATE (55–70%)
GOLD CAKE DUST (EDIBLE)

TIPS AND TRICKS

Look for edible gold cake dust in your local food store or online. Should you prefer not to use cognac or rum in the truffles, feel free to substitute with coffee or espresso.

Chop the chocolate. In a deep and heavy pan (about 9 inches in diameter), combine the heavy cream and sugar and bring to boil. Take the pan off the heat and add the chopped chocolate. Melt the chocolate while stirring with a whisk. Incorporate the butter in small pieces. Then add the brandy or rum to taste and keep stirring until the mixture is smooth. Pour the mixture onto a tray that measures about 6 x 8 inches.

Let the mixture cool then cover the tray with plastic wrap and place in a refrigerator until set, for about 2 to 3 hours, or until you can shape the mixture into balls. One tablespoon of chocolate mixture is enough for approximately one truffle. Place the truffles on a plate, cover them with plastic wrap, and place them in the fridge until they are completely set.

Prepare the topping by melting the chocolate (see page 16) and let it cool but not set. Dip the truffles in the melted chocolate one by one with the help of a fork or a toothpick. Place the truffles on a tray covered with parchment paper and put them back into the fridge to set. When the truffles are ready to serve, sprinkle them with the edible gold dust.

BUTTERNUT CUPS

MAKES 10 CUPS

INGREDIENTS
5¼ OZ CHOPPED DARK CHOCOLATE (55–70%), DIVIDED
⅓ CUP + 1 TBSP PEANUT BUTTER (STORE-BOUGHT OR HOMEMADE, SEE PAGE 102)
3½ OZ CHOPPED MILK CHOCOLATE
FINELY CHOPPED PEANUTS (ENOUGH FOR 10 BUTTERNUT CUPS)
SMALL CUPCAKE LINERS

Melt half of the dark chocolate (see page 16). Using a teaspoon, cover the bases and the sides of the cupcake liners with the melted chocolate. Place the liners on a tray in a cool place until the chocolate is set (about 20 minutes). Melt the rest of the chocolate. Add an additional thin layer of chocolate to the liners to cover each liner evenly with the chocolate. Put the liners back into the fridge to cool for another 20 minutes. Meanwhile, melt the peanut butter in a small heavy saucepan while stirring. Let the peanut butter cool but make sure it doesn't set, then divide it between the liners. Put liners back into the fridge and allow to set for another 20 minutes.

Melt the milk chocolate (see page 16) and let it cool but not set. Divide the chocolate evenly between the liners, garnish with the chopped nuts, and put the cups back into the fridge to cool and set. Take the cups out of the fridge one by one, and carefully pull off the paper liners. Store them in the fridge until ready to serve.

TIPS AND TRICKS
Use double cupcake liners if you think that the single liners are too thin and unsteady to handle. It works well to divide the melted dark chocolate, the peanut butter, and the milk chocolate into three layers in mini muffin tins if you prefer to do so. It's easier, and the cups will be just as delicious!

MINT KISSES

MAKES 50 PIECES

INGREDIENTS
1 EGG WHITE
4–5 DROPS PEPPERMINT OIL
1½ CUPS POWDERED SUGAR
2¾ OZ DARK CHOCOLATE (55–70%)

Beat the egg whites until they hold stiff peaks and add the drops of peppermint oil. Add the powdered sugar (using a sieve or sifter) and whisk the mixture until it's shiny and smooth. Fill a piping bag with the mixture and pipe flat rounds on a cookie sheet covered with parchment paper. Leave the rounds to dry overnight at room temperature. Melt the chocolate (see page 16) and pour the melted chocolate into a cone made of parchment paper. Pipe a small round of chocolate in the middle of each peppermint round and let the chocolate cool until it's set.

TIPS AND TRICKS
Mint kisses are perfect Christmas candies and a "must" for your Christmas dessert table!

CARAMEL POPCORN

with pecans

INGREDIENTS

¾ CUPS + 1 TSP MUSCOVADO
BROWN SUGAR (LIGHT OR DARK)
1 PINCH OF VANILLA SUGAR (OR:
4–6 DROPS OF VANILLA EXTRACT)
⅓ + 1 TBSP CUP GOLDEN SYRUP
3 TBSP BUTTER
¼ TSP BAKING POWDER
2¾ OZ POPPED POPCORN
⅓CUP + 1 TBSP PECAN NUTS
FLAKY SEA SALT

In a saucepan combine sugar, vanilla, syrup, and butter. Heat the mixture gently while stirring until the sugar has melted. Continue to cook for another 2 to 3 minutes until the caramel begins to thicken. Stir in the baking powder, then take the pan off the heat and immediately add the popcorn and the nuts. Turn them in the sugar mixture using a large spoon, making sure to completely cover the popcorn and nuts with the caramel. Salt the popcorn to taste.

POWDERY CINNAMON POPCORN

with marshmallows and chocolate

INGREDIENTS

2 TBSP GRANULATED SUGAR
1 TSP GROUND CINNAMON
3 TBSP COCOA POWDER
2 PINCHES OF SALT
2 ¾ OZ POPPED POPCORN, OR ENOUGH
TO COVER A LARGE COOKIE SHEET
CUP + 1 TSP MINI
MARSHMALLOWS
⅓ CUP + 1 TBSP CHOCOLATE CHIPS
(MILK OR DARK CHOCOLATE)

Heat the oven to 350°F. In a large bowl, combine the sugar, cinnamon, cocoa powder, then add the pinches of salt. Spread the popcorn on a cookie sheet covered with parchment paper. Toast the popcorn in the lower part of the oven for 5 to 8 minutes. Gently add the warm popcorn to the cocoa mixture. Finally add the marshmallows and the chocolate chips.

SRIRACHA POPCORN

sweet and spicy

INGREDIENTS

¾ CUP + 1 TSP GRANULATED SUGAR
⅓ CUP + 1 TBSP LIGHT OR GOLDEN SYRUP
3 TBSP SRIRACHA SAUCE
3 TBSP BUTTER
¼ TSP BAKING POWDER
2¾ OZ POPPED POPCORN
FLAKY SEA SALT & GROUND PAPRIKA,
TO TASTE

Heat the oven to 350°F. In a saucepan, combine the sugar, syrup, Sriracha sauce, and butter. Heat the mixture while stirring until the sugar has melted. Heat for another 2 to 3 minutes until the mixture has thickened. Add the baking powder and take the pan off the heat and immediately add the popcorn.

With the help of a large spoon, fold in the popcorn, making sure that it's completely covered with the sugar and syrup mixture. Spread out the popcorn on a cookie sheet covered with parchment baking paper and toast in the lower part of the oven for 5 to 8 minutes. Let the popcorn cool and then break it into pieces. Sprinkle with the flaky sea salt and ground paprika to taste.

FINE ORANGE CAKE

MAKES 1 CAKE, 6 TO 8 PIECES

INGREDIENTS
1 TBSP BUTTER TO GREASE THE PAN
½ CUP OF BLANCHED SHAVED ALMONDS

CAKE
1⅓ STICKS (5.25 OZ)
BUTTER AT ROOM TEMPERATURE
¾ CUP + 1 TSP GRANULATED SUGAR
2 EGGS
ORANGE ZEST FROM 1
THOROUGHLY WASHED ORANGE
¼ CUP FRESHLY SQUEEZED
ORANGE JUICE
1¼ CUPS ALL-PURPOSE FLOUR
1 TSP BAKING POWDER

Heat the oven to 350°F. Grease a round cake pan (that holds about 1.6 quarts) and cover the base and sides with blanched shaved almonds. Cream the butter and sugar with an electric mixer. Add one egg at a time and continue mixing. Add the orange zest to the batter, and then add the orange juice and keep mixing until you have a smooth batter.

Next, mix the flour and baking powder, add to the batter, and continue mixing. Pour the batter into the pan and bake for about 40 minutes until the cake is baked through, or until a toothpick inserted into the center of the cake comes out clean. Allow the cake to cool completely on a wire rack.

CHRISTMAS CAKE

with brown sugar frosting and oranges

MAKES 8 TO 10 PIECES

INGREDIENTS

2 ORANGE CAKE ROUNDS (PAGE 35)
CARAMELIZED ORANGES (PAGE 39)

FROSTING

3 TBSP BUTTER
1 TBSP GRANULATED SUGAR
2 TBSP LIGHT BROWN MUSCOVADO SUGAR
2 TBSP "WHITE" OR GOLDEN SYRUP
⅓ CUP + 1 TBSP CRÈME FRAÎCHE
2¾–3¼ CUPS POWDERED SUGAR
2 PINCHES OF FLAKY SEA SALT

GARNISH

ROSEMARY TWIGS
POWDERED SUGAR

Bake the cakes as described in the previous recipe on page 35. Make the caramelized oranges (page 39) and divide the slices after they've been frozen.

TO MAKE THE FROSTING:

In a small pan, melt the butter and add the granulated sugar, the brown sugar, and the syrup, and stir until the sugar melts. Add the crème fraîche. Turn out the mixture into a deep bowl, sift in the powdered sugar, and mix it by stirring vigorously. Let the frosting cool down but not cool completely or set.

TO ASSEMBLE THE CAKE:

Place one of the cakes on a serving platter and spread ½ of the frosting on top of the cake. Place the second cake on top and spread the rest of the frosting on the second cake. Garnish with the caramelized orange slices and add some rosemary twigs. Finally, sprinkle the top with some powdered sugar using a duster or sieve.

TIPS AND TRICKS

This very festive cake can be served with hot Christmas drinks (e.g., Swedish mulled wine called "Glögg") or with coffee. If you'd like to make a smaller cake, use one cake and make half the frosting.

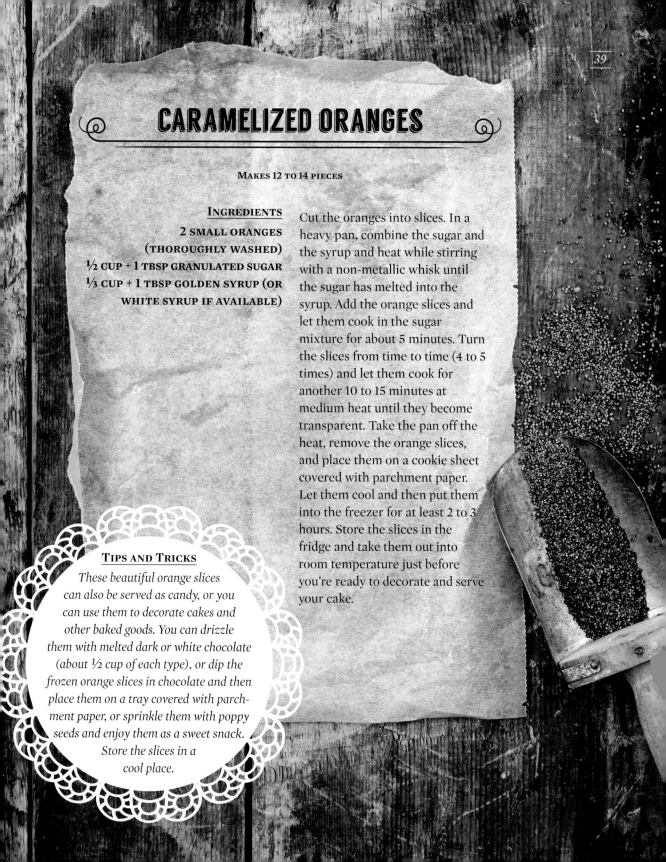

CARAMELIZED ORANGES

MAKES 12 TO 14 PIECES

INGREDIENTS
**2 SMALL ORANGES
(THOROUGHLY WASHED)
½ CUP + 1 TBSP GRANULATED SUGAR
⅓ CUP + 1 TBSP GOLDEN SYRUP (OR
WHITE SYRUP IF AVAILABLE)**

Cut the oranges into slices. In a heavy pan, combine the sugar and the syrup and heat while stirring with a non-metallic whisk until the sugar has melted into the syrup. Add the orange slices and let them cook in the sugar mixture for about 5 minutes. Turn the slices from time to time (4 to 5 times) and let them cook for another 10 to 15 minutes at medium heat until they become transparent. Take the pan off the heat, remove the orange slices, and place them on a cookie sheet covered with parchment paper. Let them cool and then put them into the freezer for at least 2 to 3 hours. Store the slices in the fridge and take them out into room temperature just before you're ready to decorate and serve your cake.

TIPS AND TRICKS
These beautiful orange slices can also be served as candy, or you can use them to decorate cakes and other baked goods. You can drizzle them with melted dark or white chocolate (about ½ cup of each type), or dip the frozen orange slices in chocolate and then place them on a tray covered with parchment paper, or sprinkle them with poppy seeds and enjoy them as a sweet snack. Store the slices in a cool place.

DATE AND WALNUT POPS

MAKES 15 POPS

INGREDIENTS
7 OZ SEEDLESS DATES
CUP + 1 TBSP WALNUTS
2 TBSP RUNNY HONEY
3 TBSP FINELY CHOPPED PISTACHIOS
3 TBSP TOASTED SESAME SEEDS
15 CAKE POP STICKS

Finely chop the dates and the walnuts either by hand or in a blender with a steel blade. Mix the dates and the walnuts with the honey in a deep bowl. Shape 15 round balls of the mixture by hand and roll them in the chopped pistachios and sesame seeds. Make sure you press the balls into the chopped nuts so that they stick properly to the surface of the balls. Insert a cake pop stick into each ball.

TIPS AND TRICKS

Buy soft, juicy, and preferably fresh dates if you can get them. These "healthy snacks" can be made well ahead and be stored in a container with a lid. If you don't serve the pops immediately, insert the pop sticks just before you're ready to serve them. Alternatively, you can serve them just as they are without pop sticks.

TCHAIKOVSKY BALLS

MAKES 12 BALLS

INGREDIENTS
4½ OZ NOUGAT
(STORE-BOUGHT)
1 SHEET OF PINK MARZIPAN
(7 OZ) (SEE TIP BELOW)
5¼ OZ DARK CHOCOLATE
(55–70%)

Cut the nougat into 12 squares and roll them into even-sized balls. Cut out small circles of the marzipan sheet to fit over the nougat and pinch and stretch the marzipan around the balls to make sure they are well covered. Roll the balls with your hands until they are smooth. Melt the chocolate (page 16) and let it cool but not set. Dip the balls one by one in the chocolate with the help of a fork. Let the balls rest for a while by placing them on a platter or cookie sheet covered with parchment paper. Leave the chocolate balls to set. Store in a cool place.

TIPS AND TRICKS
This recipe is inspired by the classic Mozart marzipan balls. The difference is that I'm using pink marzipan instead of plain marzipan, and I've excluded alcohol as a flavor to make them more child-friendly. Pink marzipan is available in specialty stores and online.

RASPBERRY AND ALMOND CARAMEL LOLLIPOPS

MAKES 20 LOLLIPOPS

INGREDIENTS

¾ CUP + 1 TSP HEAVY CREAM
¾ CUP + 1 TSP GRANULATED SUGAR
¾ CUP + 1 TSP GOLDEN SUGAR SYRUP
3–4 TBSP RASPBERRY PURÉE
3 TBSP FINELY CHOPPED ALMONDS
3 TBSP BUTTER AT ROOM TEMPERATURE
CANDY/FOOD THERMOMETER
20 LOLLIPOP STICKS

Cut out 20 squares of parchment paper approximately 5 x 5 inches and make them into cone shapes. Seal them with tape and place the cones in a glass or in a special stand for cones (see picture). In a heavy stainless pan, combine cream, sugar, syrup, and the raspberry purée while stirring until the sugar has melted. Keep stirring occasionally until the candy/food thermometer reaches 248°F (120°C). Add the chopped almonds and the butter and gently fill the cones with the caramel mixture. Stick the lollipop sticks into the middle of the cones and leave to cool.

TIPS AND TRICKS

Alternatively, you can make individual caramels using small cupcake liners (this recipe is enough for 40 caramels). If you choose to make the cones, you can decorate them with festive stickers, pictures, or ribbons (see picture).

"ICE" CHOCOLATE

MAKES 30 PIECES

INGREDIENTS
30 MINI CUPCAKE LINERS
3.5 OZ EXTRA VIRGIN SOLID COCONUT OIL
3.5 OZ DARK CHOCOLATE (55–70%)
HIMALAYAN PINK SALT FOR DECORATION

Place the liners on a tray. Melt the coconut oil in a heavy saucepan. Take the pan off the heat and add the chocolate. Let the chocolate melt while stirring. Divide the melted chocolate evenly between the 30 liners and decorate them with a little pink salt. Let them set in the fridge.

TIPS AND TRICKS
To add flavor to the Ice Chocolate cups, you can add citrus peel, finely chopped nuts, cinnamon, cardamom, chilis, salt, peppermint oil, or finely crushed candy canes.

CHRISTMAS GINGER CAKE TRUFFLES

Makes 10 truffles

Ingredients
1 small sponge cake (store-bought or homemade, about 12.5 oz)
Gingerbread spice, to taste
3.5 oz (approx.) cream cheese, divided
7 oz white chocolate

Garnish
Granulated sugar
Sliced red and green glazed cherries

Mash the sponge cake with a fork in a large mixing bowl, then mix it with the gingerbread spice and 2/3 of the cream cheese. Add the rest of the cream cheese in parts until the mixture can be shaped into balls. Divide the mixture into 10 parts and shape the truffles. Let them cool for about 30 minutes, or until they are set.

Melt the chocolate (see page 16) and let the chocolate cool but not set. Dip the truffles in the melted chocolate with the help of a fork or a toothpick and place the finished balls on a tray lined with parchment paper. Leave them to cool until they're almost set before rolling them in the granulated sugar. Garnish with the sliced glazed cherries.

CHRISTMAS PARFAIT

with caramel sauce and cashew brittle

MAKES 6 TO 8 SERVINGS

INGREDIENTS
PARFAIT
3⅓ CUPS HEAVY CREAM
8 EGG YOLKS
1 TSP GROUND CINNAMON
1 TSP GROUND CARDAMOM
1 CUP + 1 TSP GRANULATED SUGAR

TOPPING
1 SERVING CARAMEL SAUCE OR
CHOCOLATE SAUCE (SEE PAGE 52)
½ SERVING CASHEW BRITTLE
(SEE PAGE 12)

With an electric mixer, beat the cream to soft peaks in a deep bowl. In a separate bowl, combine the egg yolks, cinnamon, cardamom, and sugar, and process with the mixer until the batter has thickened and turned white and creamy. Fold the whipped cream into the egg yolk mixture and blend everything gently until the mixture is smooth. Pour the Parfait mixture into a glass dish or a Bundt cake mold (approximately 2 quarts).

Cover the dish with a lid or plastic wrap. Place the dish in the freezer for at least 24 hours. Before serving the Parfait, drop the mold or pan quickly into hot water and invert it onto a serving plate. Store it in the fridge for about 30 minutes, and just before serving, garnish with the caramel or chocolate sauce and crushed cashew brittle.

TIPS AND TRICKS
The Christmas Parfait is simply divine served with caramel sauce and the homemade Brittle. Crush the Brittle into equal sizes and serve any leftovers as candy. The parfait will be just as delicious to serve with chocolate sauce (see page 52).

CARAMEL SAUCE

MAKES 1¼ CUPS

INGREDIENTS

1 CUP + 1 TSP HEAVY CREAM
3 TBSP GRANULATED
SUGAR
¼ CUP GOLDEN SYRUP
1 TBSP BUTTER
FLAKY SEA SALT,
IF DESIRED

In a saucepan, combine cream, sugar, and syrup. Heat while stirring and keep the heat at medium high without a lid until the sauce has thickened and become light brown (about 10 minutes). Take the pan off the heat and add the butter. Add a pinch of flaky sea salt if you like.

TIPS AND TRICKS

The caramel sauce can be served cold, as a topping for cakes or ice cream, or warm over frozen berries.

CHOCOLATE SAUCE

MAKES 1¼ CUPS

INGREDIENTS

⅓ CUP + 1 TBSP GRANULATED SUGAR
⅓ CUP + 1 TBSP COCOA POWDER
½ PINCH OF SALT
⅓ CUP + 1 TSP WATER

In a saucepan, combine sugar, cocoa powder, and salt. Add the water in two or three parts and keep stirring to keep the sauce smooth. Heat the sauce while stirring and let it simmer while you continue stirring occasionally until it's thick and glossy. Let cool.

TIPS AND TRICKS

For a stronger taste, mix the cream with 1 teaspoon instant coffee granules.

BUTTER "KOLA" CARAMELS

MAKES 50 PIECES

INGREDIENTS
3.5 OZ BUTTER (7 TBSP)
¾ CUP + 1 TSP HEAVY CREAM
1¼ CUPS GRANULATED SUGAR
⅓ CUP + 1 TBSP GOLDEN SYRUP
1 TBSP VANILLA SUGAR, OR
2 TSP VANILLA EXTRACT
1 PINCH OF FLAKY SEA SALT
CANDY/FOOD THERMOMETER

In a heavy stainless saucepan or enamel coated cast iron pan, melt the butter gently. Add the cream, sugar, syrup, and vanilla. Heat while stirring until the sugar has melted. Keep the caramel at medium heat without a lid until the temperature on your food thermometer reaches 255°F (124°C).

Add the flaky sea salt and turn out the mixture onto a long cookie sheet or tray lined with parchment paper. Let it cool and set somewhat. Cut with a sharp knife or scissors into 50 pieces.

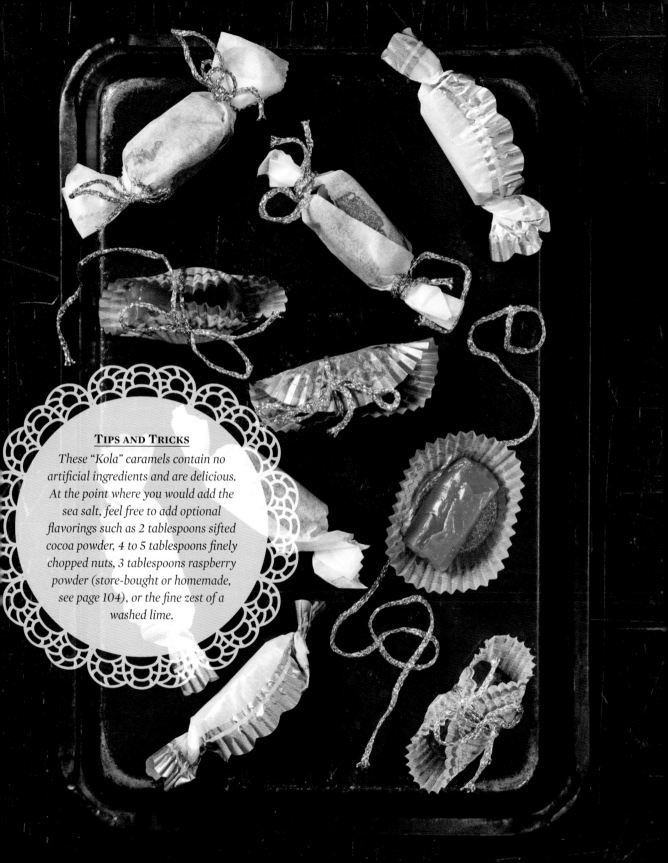

TIPS AND TRICKS

These "Kola" caramels contain no artificial ingredients and are delicious. At the point where you would add the sea salt, feel free to add optional flavorings such as 2 tablespoons sifted cocoa powder, 4 to 5 tablespoons finely chopped nuts, 3 tablespoons raspberry powder (store-bought or homemade, see page 104), or the fine zest of a washed lime.

BUTTER "*KNACK*" CARAMELS

with nuts

INGREDIENTS

50 CANDY WRAPPERS OR
MINI CUPCAKE LINERS
⅓ CUP + 1 TBSP TOASTED HAZELNUTS
¾ CUP + 1 TSP HEAVY CREAM
½ CUP + 1 TBSP GOLDEN SYRUP
¾ CUP + 1 TSP GRANULATED SUGAR
CANDY/FOOD THERMOMETER

Place the candy wrappers on a cookie sheet or a tray. Finely chop the nuts. In a heavy stainless saucepan, combine the cream and syrup and bring to a boil while stirring. Add the sugar and stir well until it's melted. Heat the mixture until it reaches 255°F (124°C). Add the chopped nuts and then quickly spoon or pour the mixture into the candy wrappers and allow to cool. When the candies have cooled down, move them to the fridge to set completely.

TIPS AND TRICKS

The hazelnuts can be substituted for most other nuts (almonds, peanuts, or salted or unsalted cashew nuts). If you'd like your "Knäck" to have a stronger caramel flavor, then replace ½ of the granulated sugar with brown sugar. Store the "Knäck" in a cool place, preferably in a tin in layers lined with parchment paper.

COCONUT POPCORN

INGREDIENTS

¾–1¼ CUPS UNSWEETENED COCONUT FLAKES
4–5 CUPS POPPED POPCORN
1–2 TBSP SOLID COCONUT OIL
3 TBSP AGAVE NECTAR
CHILI FLAKES, TO TASTE
FLAKY SEA SALT, TO TASTE

Heat the oven to 350°F. Spread out the coconut flakes evenly on a cookie sheet lined with parchment paper and toast in the middle of the oven until the flakes are light brown, making sure that they don't burn. Spread out the popped popcorn on a cookie sheet lined with parchment paper and toast in the lower part of the oven for 5 to 8 minutes.

In a small saucepan, melt the coconut oil. In a separate bowl, carefully combine the warm popcorn with the syrup and the coconut oil. Fold in the toasted coconut flakes. Add the chili flakes and the flaky sea salt to taste.

TIPS AND TRICKS

It's fun to use interesting vintage tins for the popcorn. Check out your local flea markets for tins that won't break the bank.

ICE CREAM AND MERINGUE BOMB

MAKES 8 PIECES

INGREDIENTS
3¼ CUPS STRAWBERRY SORBET
2 CUPS (APPROX.) BLUEBERRY SORBET
2 CUPS (APPROX.) PISTACHIO ICE CREAM
3 EGG WHITES
½ CUP + 1 TBSP GRANULATED SUGAR
1 THIN ROUND SPONGE CAKE (HOMEMADE
OR STORE-BOUGHT)
CULINARY BLOW TORCH FOR CARAMELIZING
THE MERINGUE

Cover the inside of a deep round glass mold or bowl (holding about 2 quarts) with plastic wrap. Layer the strawberry sorbet, the blueberry sorbet, and the pistachio ice cream in the bowl. Cover with plastic wrap and place in the freezer for 5 to 6 hours or overnight. Quickly dip the bowl in hot water just before you're ready for the next step. Turn out the ice cream onto a cookie sheet lined with parchment paper and freeze for at least another 2 hours.

Beat the egg whites until the whites hold a stiff peak. Add half of the sugar and continue to beat making sure that the mixture stays stiff. Add the rest of the sugar a few tablespoons at a time and keep beating for another 2 to 3 minutes, until the mixture is thick and glossy.

Place the round sponge cake on a serving plate. Remove the plastic wrap and spoon the ice cream on top of the sponge cake and cut the cake to size if it overlaps your ice cream mold. Spread the meringue mixture like a tight helmet around the ice cream and sponge cake. Use a culinary blow torch to gently caramelize the meringue until it's beautifully browned but not burned. Serve immediately!

TIPS AND TRICKS

You can substitute the suggested ice creams and sorbet with your favorite flavors and colors. Feel free to decorate with sparklers to make the cake look extra festive for the holidays.

FIG TRUFFLES

filled with chocolate and cognac

MAKES 12 PIECES

INGREDIENTS
12 SMALL DRIED FIGS
1¾ OZ MILK CHOCOLATE
1 TBSP CRÈME FRAÎCHE
1 TBSP COGNAC

FOR THE TOPPING
3.5 OZ DARK CHOCOLATE
SIFTED COCOA POWDER FOR DUSTING

Cut an opening for the filling at the base of each fig with the help of a small sharp knife.

Chop the milk chocolate. In a small saucepan, heat the crème fraîche and add the cognac while stirring. Take the pan off the heat and add the chopped chocolate, letting it melt while stirring. When the chocolate has melted, take the pan off the heat and let the mixture cool for about 30 minutes at room temperature, making sure that it doesn't set completely.

Fill the figs with the chocolate mixture with the help of a small spoon or pastry bag. Place the finished figs on a tray or cookie sheet lined with parchment paper and transfer to the fridge for approximately 1 hour to set. Melt the dark chocolate (see page 16), and drizzle it over the figs. Let the figs set in the fridge for about 30 minutes before serving. Sprinkle with the sifted cocoa powder and serve the figs at room temperature.

TIPS AND TRICKS
Look for small, floured dried figs in your local supermarket or in Middle Eastern stores.

"DAIM" ICE FLOATS

INGREDIENTS
¾ CUP + 1 TSP GRANULATED SUGAR
¾ CUP + 1 TSP GOLDEN SYRUP
¾ CUP + 1 TSP HEAVY CREAM
1 TBSP BUTTER

OPTIONAL:
THE ZEST OF ONE LIME, WASHED
7 OZ CHOCOLATE (MILK OR DARK)
FOOD/CANDY THERMOMETER

Line a cookie sheet with parchment paper and draw a circle on the paper (approximately 9 inches in diameter). In a saucepan, combine the sugar, syrup, and cream and heat while stirring with a whisk until the sugar has melted. Heat the mixture at medium heat to 257°F (125°C). Take the pan off the heat and stir in the butter and the optional lime zest. Pour the mixture onto the parchment paper and spread it out to cover the circle that you drew. Let the mixture cool and set.

Melt the chocolate (see page 16) and let it cool but not set completely. Spread the chocolate over the "DAIM" caramel with a knife with a wide blade. Let it cool and set completely. Place the finished product in the fridge for about 1 hour, then break it into pieces of desired sizes.

TIPS AND TRICKS
You can break the "DAIM" bars into larger pieces or smaller bite-size pieces. It doesn't matter how big or small they are. Regardless of the size, you can't stop eating them!

ALMOND AND PEAR GALETTE

INGREDIENTS

**7 OZ ALMOND PASTE
(STORE-BOUGHT)
3 TBSP MUSCOVADO BROWN
SUGAR (LIGHT OR DARK)
1 TBSP MELTED BUTTER
2 EGGS
PUFF PASTRY (1 SHEET,
STORE-BOUGHT)
2 PEARS (PREFERABLY BROWN)
JUICE OF ½ LEMON
6–8 TBSP POWDERED SUGAR
1 SMALL EGG**

TIPS AND TRICKS

*Sifting the powdered sugar over
the galette in regular intervals
while it's baking is the key to
achieving a perfectly caramelized final product. Serve the
galette sliced into thin slices
together with a hot Christmas
drink such as Swedish "Glögg"
(Mulled Wine).*

Beat the almond paste with the brown sugar and butter with an electric mixer. Add the eggs one at a time. Roll out the puff pastry and press it into a round pie dish (roughly 9.5 inches in diameter). Trim out the edges and prick the edges and the bottom of the dough with a fork. Spread the almond paste mixture over the puff pastry sheet and let rest for about 15 minutes. Heat the oven to 350°F.

Cut the pears into quarters and remove the seeds. Then cut the pear quarters into thin slices. Squeeze the lemon juice over the pears to stop them from darkening. Place the pear slices on top of the almond mixture and sift 2 tablespoons powdered sugar over the pears. Bake in the lower part of the oven for about 40 minutes until the pastry has browned and the pears are soft. Sift 2 to 3 tablespoons of powdered sugar over the pears 2 to 3 times while the galette is baking in the oven. Top with more powdered sugar before serving the cake, if desired.

FINNISH CHRISTMAS STARS

MAKES 6 STARS

INGREDIENTS

1 PACKET OF ROLLED OUT PUFF PASTRY
(STORE-BOUGHT)
⅓ CUP + 1 TBSP DRIED PRUNE PRESERVES
(STORE-BOUGHT OR HOMEMADE, SEE PAGE 71)
1 TBSP (APPROX.) POWDERED SUGAR

Heat the oven to 435°F. Roll out the puff pastry sheet and place it on a cookie sheet covered with parchment paper. Cut the dough into 4 x 4-inch squares with a sharp knife. Remove any excess dough. Make a cut from corner to corner towards the middle of the pastry sheet, but not all the way through.

Place a spoonful of prune preserves in the middle of each square. Fold the corners like a windmill. Bake in the middle of the oven for about 12 minutes, or until the puff pastry is nicely browned. Sift the stars with powdered sugar before serving.

TIPS AND TRICKS

Dried prune preserves have a drier consistency than other preserves, such as plum preserve, and will not seep out from the stars while they are baking. Prune preserves can be found in specialty stores or online, but is easy to make yourself (see page 71). This Christmas dessert usually proves to be very popular.

DRIED PRUNE PRESERVES

Makes about 1 cup

Ingredients
½ cup (approx.) water
1 packet/bag of pitted
dried prunes (approx. 7 oz)

In a saucepan, heat the water to boiling point. Add the prunes and simmer until the prunes are soft and mushy. Add water if needed. Take the pan off the heat and mix with a handheld blender until the mixture is smooth.

NOUGAT SLICES

with almonds and chocolate

INGREDIENTS

1 CUP TOASTED SALTED ALMONDS
(SEE TIP BELOW)
10 OZ DARK CHOCOLATE (55–70%)
17.5 OZ NOUGAT (STORE-BOUGHT,
PREFERABLY ODENSE VIENNESE
NOUGAT), DIVIDED

Line a cookie sheet (about 6 x 8 inches) with parchment paper. Chop half of the almonds coarsely and keep the rest for the topping. In a saucepan, melt the chocolate (see page 16). Cut the nougat into smaller pieces and add half to the pan, allowing it to melt into the chocolate. Mix until the batter is smooth and add the chopped almonds.

Turn out the batter onto the cookie sheet or tray and let it cool in the fridge to set for about one hour. Melt the rest of the nougat and pour it over the top of the mixture that has been cooling in the fridge. Garnish with the rest of the almonds and put the cookie sheet / tray back into the fridge to set. Store in the fridge and cut the nougat into slices before serving.

TIPS AND TRICKS

The luxurious Marcona almonds work perfectly with nougat and chocolate (can be found in specialty stores and online). You can also use regular blanched salted almonds, or perhaps smoked almonds if they are available. If you'd like to use regular unsalted blanched almonds, then first toast them in a dry frying pan.

PEANUT FUDGE

Makes 16 pieces

Ingredients
3 cups powdered sugar
1 tsp vanilla sugar or
½ tsp vanilla extract
5.25 oz butter (1⅓ sticks)
⅓ cup heavy cream
1½ cups peanut butter
(store-bought or
homemade, see page 102
for recipe)

Cover a cookie sheet or tray (about 6 x 8 inches) with parchment paper. In a mixing bowl that can withstand heat, combine powdered sugar and vanilla.

In a saucepan, combine the butter, cream, and peanut butter. Gently heat the mixture on medium heat while stirring until it becomes smooth and bubbly on the surface.

Pour the mixture over the sugar and the vanilla and mix well, preferably with an electric mixer. Pour the fudge mixture onto the cookie sheet and spread it evenly with a spatula. Cover the fudge with parchment paper and press it so that surface is even. Let cool and then set in the fridge for 2 to 3 hours. Cut the fudge into pieces before serving.

PEANUT BRITTLE

dipped in chocolate

INGREDIENTS

½ CUP + 1 TBSP GOLDEN SYRUP
¼ CUP WATER
1 CUP + 1 TSP GRANULATED SUGAR
7 OZ SALTED PEANUTS
2 TBSP BUTTER AT ROOM TEMPERATURE
1 TSP BAKING POWDER
5.25 OZ MILK OR DARK CHOCOLATE
FOOD/CANDY THERMOMETER

Cover a cookie sheet with parchment paper. In a saucepan, combine the syrup and water and heat while stirring with a whisk. Add the sugar and keep cooking until the sugar has melted. Make sure you don't exceed 284°F (140°C) when heating the sugar. Add the peanuts and let the mixture simmer on medium heat until your thermometer reads 302°F (150°C).

Take the pan off the heat and stir in the butter and the baking powder. Turn the mixture onto the cookie sheet and spread it out. Let the Brittle set and then break it into pieces. Melt the chocolate (see page 16) and dip the brittle pieces in the chocolate, making sure that only one side is covered by the chocolate.

TIPS AND TRICKS

These sweet but salty Brittles are simply irresistible! You can make them well in advance of the holidays. Store them at room temperature in a tin or on a plate with parchment paper between the layers to avoid the pieces sticking to each other.

WHITE CHOCOLATE TRUFFLES

coated with powdered sugar and flavored with lime

MAKES 25 TRUFFLES

INGREDIENTS

9 OZ WHITE CHOCOLATE WITH LIME FLAVOR (OR, IF UNAVAILABLE, ADD THE ZEST OF ONE LIME TO PLAIN MILK CHOCOLATE)
½ CUP HEAVY CREAM
3 TBSP POWDERED SUGAR

TOPPING

POWDERED SUGAR, TO TASTE

Break the chocolate into pieces. In a saucepan, combine the cream and the powdered sugar and bring to boil while stirring. Take the pan off the heat, add the chocolate pieces, and let the mixture stand for 5 minutes. Mix with a balloon whisk until the chocolate has melted.

Next, turn the chocolate mixture onto a tray covered with parchment paper, and let it set in the fridge for about 1 hour, or until the mixture has set enough for you to shape it into truffles. When the truffles are ready, coat them with the powdered sugar, and store in a cool place.

TIPS AND TRICKS

These truffles are easy to make and are great hostess gifts. Put them into glass jars and decorate with festive ribbons, cards, ornaments, etc.

CHRISTMAS ROCKY ROAD

Ingredients

7 oz Swedish ginger thins
(e.g., 1½ boxes of "Anna's ginger thins")
1 cup toasted hazelnuts
9 oz dark chocolate
9 oz milk chocolate
6.2 oz butter (approx. 1½ sticks)
4 tbsp runny honey
5.25 oz (1 cup) red glazed cherries
4.5 oz mini marshmallows

Put the ginger thins in a plastic bag and crush them into small pieces with a rolling pin. Chop the hazelnuts and the chocolate coarsely. In a saucepan, melt the butter and add the chopped chocolate pieces. Take the pan off the heat and let it cool for 5 minutes. Keep stirring the chocolate until it's melted completely. Stir in the honey. Transfer the mixture to a bowl, and add the crushed ginger thins and the hazelnuts. Mix well and then fold in the glazed cherries and the marshmallows. Turn out the finished mixture onto a rectangular tray or small cookie sheet covered with plastic wrap or parchment paper.

Cover the rocky road with plastic wrap and store in a cool place for 3 to 4 hours or until the mixture has set enough to be turned out on a plate and cut into pieces. Store the rocky road pieces in the fridge and take them out into room temperature about 10 minutes before serving.

Tips and Tricks

Serve your rocky road pieces on a festive serving plate and decorate with holiday ornaments.

RUM AND RAISIN TRUFFLES

MAKES 20 TO 25 TRUFFLES

INGREDIENTS
½ CUP GOLDEN RAISINS
2 TBSP DARK RUM
9 OZ DARK CHOCOLATE
½ CUP HEAVY CREAM
1 OZ / ¼ STICK BUTTER AT
ROOM TEMPERATURE
COCOA POWDER OR
POWDERED SUGAR

Chop the raisins and mix them with the rum in a deep bowl. Chop the chocolate. In a small and deep saucepan (about 9 inches in diameter), heat the cream. Take the pan off the heat and add the chocolate, then mix with a handheld electric mixer until the chocolate has melted. Mix in the butter, and then the raisin and rum mixture. Turn out the truffle mixture onto a tray or cookie sheet covered with parchment paper (about 6 x 8 inches) and let it cool.

Cover with plastic wrap and let it cool for 2 to 3 hours until the truffle mixture has set, or until it can be formed into round balls. Use a teaspoon to measure the amount of mixture you'll need for one truffle and place the finished truffles on a tray covered with parchment paper. Sift cocoa powder or powdered sugar over the truffles to finish them off.

TIPS AND TRICKS
Rum and raisins go very well together with chocolate, but you can also substitute the raisins with finely grated dates that are available in specialty stores.

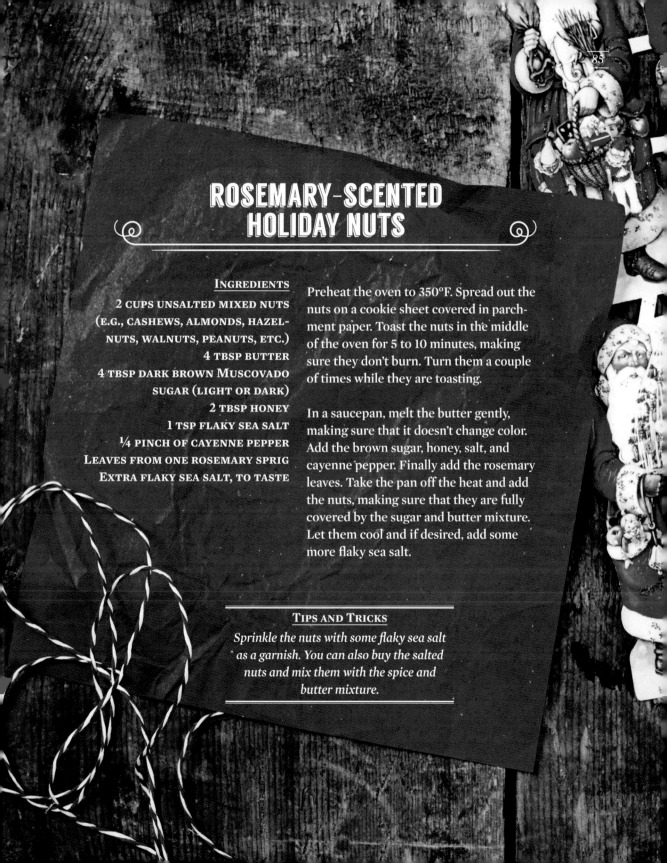

ROSEMARY-SCENTED HOLIDAY NUTS

INGREDIENTS

**2 CUPS UNSALTED MIXED NUTS
(E.G., CASHEWS, ALMONDS, HAZEL-
NUTS, WALNUTS, PEANUTS, ETC.)
4 TBSP BUTTER
4 TBSP DARK BROWN MUSCOVADO
SUGAR (LIGHT OR DARK)
2 TBSP HONEY
1 TSP FLAKY SEA SALT
¼ PINCH OF CAYENNE PEPPER
LEAVES FROM ONE ROSEMARY SPRIG
EXTRA FLAKY SEA SALT, TO TASTE**

Preheat the oven to 350°F. Spread out the nuts on a cookie sheet covered in parchment paper. Toast the nuts in the middle of the oven for 5 to 10 minutes, making sure they don't burn. Turn them a couple of times while they are toasting.

In a saucepan, melt the butter gently, making sure that it doesn't change color. Add the brown sugar, honey, salt, and cayenne pepper. Finally add the rosemary leaves. Take the pan off the heat and add the nuts, making sure that they are fully covered by the sugar and butter mixture. Let them cool and if desired, add some more flaky sea salt.

TIPS AND TRICKS

Sprinkle the nuts with some flaky sea salt as a garnish. You can also buy the salted nuts and mix them with the spice and butter mixture.

SAFFRON CAKE

with white chocolate frosting and cranberries

Makes 1 cake, serves approximately 8

Ingredients
1 soft saffron cake (see page 88)

Frosting
7 oz cream cheese
3 tbsp heavy cream
3.5 oz chopped white chocolate

Garnish/topping
Fresh cranberries
Powdered sugar
Fresh rosemary

First, make the Saffron Cake on page 88.

To make the frosting: In a deep bowl, process the cream cheese with an electric mixer. Heat the heavy cream in a small saucepan and add the chopped chocolate. Take the pan off the heat and mix the chocolate with the cream until the chocolate has melted.

Combine the chocolate mixture with the cream cheese and mix until it becomes fluffy and creamy. Spread the frosting on top of the Saffron Cake and garnish with fresh cranberries. Sift powdered sugar over the frosting and the cranberries and decorate with fresh rosemary sprigs.

Tips and Tricks
For this luxurious Saffron Cake, we use both fresh and dried cranberries. Use the dried cranberries for the cake and use the fresh berries for the topping. The result will be a very festive and beautiful cake for the holidays!

SOFT SAFFRON CAKE

MAKES 1 CAKE, SERVES APPROXIMATELY 8

INGREDIENTS
BREADCRUMBS, FOR
BREADING THE CAKE PAN
0.2 OZ SAFFRON
½ CUP BOILING WATER
8 OZ / 2 STICKS BUTTER AT
ROOM TEMPERATURE
1⅔ CUPS GRANULATED SUGAR
4 EGGS
2 CUPS ALL-PURPOSE FLOUR
2 TSP BAKING POWDER
½ CUP DRIED CRANBERRIES
1 TBSP ALL-PURPOSE FLOUR
1 TBSP (APPROX.) BUTTER TO
GREASE THE MOLD

TIPS AND TRICKS
*Look for soft dried cranber-
ries. Berries that are too hard
can be softened in a bowl of
boiling water for 10 minutes.
Dry the berries with a towel
before you add them to the
batter.*

Preheat the oven to 350°F. Grease a Bundt pan or other cake pan (size: about 2 quarts) and cover the greased surface with quality breadcrumbs. Mix the saffron with the boiling water in a cup and leave to infuse for about 5 minutes.

Cream the butter and sugar until it's smooth with an electric mixer. Add one egg at a time and keep mixing. Pour the water that has been infused with the saffron threads into the batter through a fine sieve. Mix the flour with the baking powder and mix well. Add the dried cranberries to the flour mixture, and then add to the batter.

Transfer the batter to a Bundt pan or other cake mold and bake in the lower part of the oven for 50 to 60 minutes or until the cake is ready. Test its readiness with a toothpick or a steel cake tester. Let the cake cool for a while before you turn it out onto a serving plate. Let cool for a little longer before serving.

RASPBERRY LOLLIPOPS

Makes 8 lollipops

Ingredients

1 DOUBLED SHEET OF
PARCHMENT PAPER
(TO FIT YOUR SHEET PAN)
1 TBSP VEGETABLE OIL
FOR BRUSHING
1 CUP + 1 TSP GRANULATED SUGAR
1½ TBSP GLUCOSE SYRUP
⅓ CUP WATER
¼ TEASPOON OF RED
FOOD COLORING
¼ TEASPOON RASPBERRY FLAVORING
EDIBLE GLITTER SPRINKLES
LOLLIPOP STICKS
FOOD / CANDY THERMOMETER

Place the double sheet of parchment paper on top of your sheet pan and brush the paper with vegetable oil. In a heavy stainless saucepan combine the sugar, glucose, and water. Heat the mixture while stirring until the sugar has melted. Add the food coloring in drops until the desired color is achieved and continue cooking in the pan with a lid for 2 to 3 minutes.

Remove the lid and continue heating the mixture until your thermometer reads 266°F (130°C). Take the pan off the heat and add the raspberry flavoring and mix well. Turn out the mixture in 8 equal rounds onto the parchment paper. Cover with the sprinkles and insert the lollipop sticks. Leave the lollipops to cool and set.

Tips and Tricks

Red lollipops are perfect to make for the holidays, but green ones are just as festive. Buy some green food coloring and feel free to add a few drops of peppermint oil if you like. I think that handmade lollipops with uneven edges are the most beautiful, but if you prefer to make yours into even shapes, you can buy molds online or in specialty stores.

SNOWBALLS

MAKES 35 TRUFFLES

INGREDIENTS
6.25 OZ WHITE CHOCOLATE
⅓ CUP + 1 TBSP HEAVY CREAM
1 CUP SHREDDED UNSWEETENED COCONUT
THE ZEST OF ONE WASHED LIME OR LEMON

GARNISH / TOPPING
SHREDDED COCONUT

Chop the chocolate. In a small saucepan, heat the heavy cream. Take the pan off the heat, add the chocolate, and let it melt while stirring. Add the shredded coconut and the zest of the lime or lemon and mix well. Let the mixture cool at room temperature and then in the fridge for 1 hour until it's set, or until it can be shaped into balls. Shape them into small truffles and roll them in the shredded coconut. Store in a cool place.

TIPS AND TRICKS
These snowballs are simply delicious with a fresh taste of citrus and loved by anyone with a sweet tooth—adults and children alike. Take the snowballs out of the fridge into room temperature, about 15 minutes before serving.

TIRAMISU TRUFFLES

MAKES 6 LARGE TRUFFLES

INGREDIENTS
8 LADY FINGERS ("SAVOIARDI" COOKIES)
3 TBSP STRONG COFFEE OR ESPRESSO
3 TBSP MARSALA WINE
4.5 OZ MASCARPONE CHEESE
3 TBSP HEAVY CREAM
1 EGG YOLK
$\frac{1}{3}$ CUP + 1 TBSP GRANULATED SUGAR
7 OZ DARK, MILK, OR WHITE CHOCOLATE

TOPPING
COCOA POWDER

Break the lady fingers into pieces and place them in a deep bowl. Combine the coffee and the marsala wine and pour the mixture over the cookies. Leave to soak for about 3 minutes and then mash the cookies with a fork. In another bowl, add the mascarpone cheese and the cream and beat the mixture until it's creamy. Combine the cookie mixture with the cheese and cream mixture. In a separate bowl, whisk the egg yolk and sugar until it's creamy, then incorporate the cookie mixture and the cheese and cream mixture.

Place the Tiramisu mixture in a square dish (8 x 8 inches). Cover with plastic wrap and cool it in the fridge for 1½ to 2 hours or until you can shape the mixture into truffles. Shape the truffles and place them on a tray or on a small cookie sheet covered with parchment paper, then leave them to set in the freezer. Melt the chocolate (see page 16). Dip the truffles one at a time into the melted chocolate and place them on a tray or small cookie sheet in the freezer for roughly 20 minutes. Let the truffles rest at room temperature for about 20 minutes before serving them, and finally dust the truffles with sifted cocoa powder.

TIPS AND TRICKS
These large and sumptuous truffles are a variation of the classic Italian dessert "Tiramisù," which literally means "Pick-me-up," and are perfect served with strong coffee or espresso. You can easily double the number of truffles if you make them smaller. Marsala wine can be substituted with whisky or another liquor of your choice.

WALNUT AND CHOCOLATE FUDGE

MAKES 16 PIECES

INGREDIENTS

5¼ OZ DARK CHOCOLATE (55–70%)
1 CUP + 1 TSP GRANULATED SUGAR
CUP LIGHT BROWN MUSCOVADO
SUGAR (LIGHT OR DARK)
1 CUP + 1 TSP HEAVY CREAM
⅓ + 1 TBSP CUP MILK
⅓ CUP + 1 TBSP GOLDEN SYRUP
½ STICK / 1.75 OZ BUTTER
⅓ CUP + 1 TBSP WALNUTS
FOOD/CANDY THERMOMETER

Chop the chocolate. Line a cookie sheet or tray (approximately 6 x 8 inches) with parchment paper. In a saucepan, combine the granulated sugar, brown sugar, cream, milk, syrup, and butter, and cook at medium heat while stirring until the sugar has melted.

Simmer the mixture to 243°F (117°C). Check with your food thermometer. Take the pan off the heat and add the chocolate. Stir the mixture until it has cooled slightly (about 3 minutes). Add the walnut halves. Turn out the fudge batter onto the tray or cookie sheet and let it set at room temperature. Cut into squares.

TIPS AND TRICKS

This chocolate fudge with walnuts is soft and creamy. You can substitute the walnuts with pecans, if you like.

WHITE CHOCOLATE BARS

with apricots and walnuts

MAKES 10 TO 12 PIECES

INGREDIENTS
10 DRIED APRICOTS
⅓ CUP OF WALNUT HALVES
10½ OZ WHITE CHOCOLATE

GARNISH
POWDERED SUGAR

Finely chop the apricots and the walnuts and melt the chocolate (see page 16). Combine the chopped apricots and nuts with the chocolate. Turn out the mixture onto a small round tray or cookie sheet covered with parchment paper.

Let cool at room temperature before covering the tray /cookie sheet with plastic wrap. Place it in the fridge for 2 to 3 hours or overnight. When you're ready to serve the bars, cut them into long strips and sift powdered sugar on top of them.

TIPS AND TRICKS

This is a very easy recipe for delicious chocolate bars with healthy ingredients such as fruits and nuts. Choose soft and juicy dried apricots if you can find them.

MERRY *CHRISTMAS

CHOCOLATE MEDALS

Makes 10 medals

Ingredients
3.5 oz dark chocolate (55–70%)
Dulce de leche (see page 102)

Topping (optional)
Pistachios
Pecans
Dried figs
Dried apricots
Raisins
Flaky sea salt
Pink peppercorns
Black sesame seeds

Make Dulce de Leche (see page 102). If you'd like to add a topping, cut whichever fruits and nuts you choose into small pieces or slices.

Melt the chocolate (see page 16). Pipe or use a small spoon to drop rounds ("medals") of the chocolate onto a tray covered with parchment paper. Add the topping mix to each medal.

Let cool in the fridge. Carefully remove the medals from the paper and make a sandwich two medals with a spoonful of Dulce the Leche in the middle. Store in a cool place before serving.

Tips and Tricks
If you love a chocolate hazelnut spread like Nutella, you can use a store-bought brand or a homemade spread instead of Dulce de Leche as a filling. (Recipe on page 102.)

DULCE DE LECHE

INGREDIENTS
1 CAN OF SWEETENED CONDENSED MILK

Place the unopened can of condensed milk in a deep saucepan and cover it completely with water by approximately 4 inches. Bring the water to boil and then let it simmer at very low heat for approximately 3 hours. Add more water from time to time to make sure that the can is completely covered throughout the cooking time. Discard the water and immerse the can in cold water for about 30 minutes. Open the can carefully and turn out the dulce de leche into a bowl. Cover with plastic wrap and let it cool completely in the fridge.

TIPS AND TRICKS
Use a timer to remind yourself to check that there is enough water to cover the can while the Dulce de Leche is cooking. Keep a close watch to make sure that the can is always covered in water; otherwise, it could explode and create a huge mess.

5-MINUTE PEANUT BUTTER

MAKES ABOUT 10 OUNCES

INGREDIENTS
1⅓ CUPS DRY ROASTED UNSALTED PEANUTS
½ CUP DRY ROASTED SALTED PEANUTS

OPTIONAL:
2–3 TBSP VEGETABLE OIL
GRANULATED SUGAR, TO TASTE
SALT, TO TASTE

For smooth peanut butter:
In a blender or food processor, process the peanuts until they are the consistency of breadcrumbs. Continue processing for about 3 minutes, until the fat from the nuts has been released. If your peanut butter seems too dry, add the vegetable oil slowly in a steady stream until the peanut butter is smooth. Add sugar and salt to taste.

TIPS AND TRICKS
To make crunchy peanut butter, follow the recipe above but reserve about ½ cup of the peanut crumbs (either coarse or smooth) and add to the peanut butter mixture at the end.

TIPS AND TRICKS

Recipe for Homemade Chocolate Hazelnut spread can be found on page 104.

HOMEMADE CHOCOLATE HAZELNUT SPREAD

Ingredients
1 CUP + 1 TSP ROASTED HAZELNUTS
¼ CUP GRANULATED SUGAR
9 OZ DARK CHOCOLATE (55–70%)
½ CUP HEAVY CREAM
½ STICK BUTTER (1.75 OZ)
1–2 PINCHES OF FLAKY SEA SALT

In a blender or food processor, process the hazelnuts and sugar. Chop the chocolate coarsely. In a saucepan, heat the cream and the sugar while stirring. Add the chocolate and let it melt while continuing to stir. Pour the chocolate mixture into the blender. Add the salt and process until smooth. Store the spread in a glass jar.

RASPBERRY POWDER

Makes 6 to 8 pops

Ingredients
2 GENEROUS CUPS FREEZE-
DRIED RASPBERRIES
(UNSWEETENED)

In a food processor or blender fitted with a steel blade, add the raspberries and blend until the raspberries turn to fine powder.

PINK SHREDDED COCONUT

Ingredients
1¼ CUPS SHREDDED
COCONUT (UNSWEETENED)
RED FOOD COLORING

Place the shredded coconut in a glass bowl and add the red food coloring in drops. Mix quickly until the coconut is evenly tinted to the color shade of your choice.

APPLE POPS WITH SPRINKLES

Makes 6 to 8 pops

Ingredients
6–8 apples (smaller variety, if possible)
7 oz chocolate (milk, dark, or pink)
6–8 apple twigs or round long pop sticks or skewers
Sprinkles, 3–4 different types

Wash and dry the apples carefully. Place them in the fridge to cool for 1 hour. Melt the chocolate (see page 16). Insert an apple twig or a round skewer or long pop stick into the top of the apples (read the tip below if you'd like to use colored twigs). Dip the apples in the melted chocolate and sprinkle with the sprinkles. Let the finished apple pops cool on a cookie sheet covered with parchment paper before serving.

Tips and Tricks

These chocolate-dipped apples with sprinkles are just as pretty as they are delicious. If you'd like your apples to look extra festive, then dip them into the three different types of chocolate. If you can't find pink chocolate, then feel free to color white chocolate by adding a drop or two of red food coloring to the melted white chocolate. Choose your favorite local sweet and juicy apple variety for this recipe, such as Cox's Orange Pippin or a similar variety. Just make sure they are not too large. If you'd like to paint the apple twigs in silver or gold, please make sure you use edible food paint.

INGREDIENTS

1⅔ CUPS ALL-PURPOSE FLOUR
¾ CUP + 1 TSP GRANULATED SUGAR
1 TSP VANILLA SUGAR OR
½ TSP VANILLA EXTRACT
2 PINCHES OF FLAKY SEA SALT
1¼ STICKS /5.25 OZ BUTTER AT
ROOM TEMPERATURE
1 EGG
3 TBSP MILK
1–1¼ CUPS DARK CHOCOLATE BUTTONS
1–1¼ CUPS WHITE CHOCOLATE BUTTONS
½–¾ CUPS OF CHOCOLATE SPRINKLES

Preheat the oven to 435°F. On a cookie sheet covered with parchment paper, spread out the flour evenly. Toast the flour in the middle of the oven for about 5 minutes, making sure that it doesn't burn. Let it cool at room temperature. In a mixing bowl, combine the sugar, vanilla, salt, and the butter divided into knobs, and process using an electric mixer. Add the flour while processing, and then the egg as you continue to process the dough. Add the milk little by little until the dough has the desired consistency. Finally add the chocolate buttons and the sprinkles to the dough. Let the dough stand in a cool place for about 30 minutes.

TIPS AND TRICKS

Is it a crazy idea to eat uncooked cookie dough? It's really delicious, and it's no wonder that eating cookie dough has become a big trend in the United States. If you can stop yourself finishing the dough immediately, then let it cool in the fridge for about 30 minutes. It's best served cold. Serve the dough in small dessert bowls or fill waffle cones with the dough and eat it like ice cream. If you prefer to bake the dough into cookies, then drop approximately 6 to 8 balls of the dough onto a cookie sheet covered with parchment paper and flatten the balls before baking them for 10 minutes in 435°F.

Please note: Consuming raw or undercooked meats, poultry, seafood, shellfish, or eggs may increase your risk of foodborne illness, especially if you have certain medical conditions.

LUXURIOUS PINK CHOCOLATE TRUFFLES

MAKES 15 TO 20 PIECES

INGREDIENTS

⅓ CUP + 1 TBSP HEAVY CREAM
3.5 OZ DARK CHOCOLATE, CHOPPED (55–70%)
1 STICK / 3.5 OZ BUTTER
⅓ CUP + 1 TBSP CUP GRANULATED SUGAR
⅓ CUP MUSCOVADO BROWN SUGAR (LIGHT OR DARK)
3 TBSP COCOA (WITH HIGH COCOA PERCENTAGE)
2½–3 CUPS ROLLED OATS

TOPPING

UNSWEETENED SHREDDED COCONUT, NATURAL OR PINK (SEE PAGE 104)

In a small saucepan, heat the heavy cream. Add the chocolate, take the pan off the heat, and stir while the chocolate is melting. In a food processor or blender fitted with a metal blade, combine the butter, granulated sugar and the brown sugar. Add the chocolate and process. Add the rolled oats and mix everything quickly, making sure not to break up the rolled oats too much. Turn out the mixture into a bowl and then shape 15 to 20 even truffles. Roll them in the shredded coconut (pink, if you prefer; see page 104). Store in a cool place.

CANDIED ORANGE PEEL

MAKES ABOUT 20 PIECES

INGREDIENTS
2 ORANGES
GRANULATED SUGAR FOR GARNISH

SYRUP
CUP + 1 TBSP GRANULATED SUGAR
CUP GOLDEN (OR WHITE) SYRUP
CUP FRESHLY SQUEEZED ORANGE
JUICE

Clean the oranges with a brush and warm water. Cut the oranges into halves and squeeze to make the fresh juice. Cover the orange halves with water and bring to boil. Turn the heat down and let simmer for 30 minutes. Place the fruit halves in a colander and let them cool. Remove all that's left of the inside of the fruit including all the white parts, and discard. Cut the peel into thick strips. In a heavy pan, combine the sugar and the freshly squeezed orange juice and heat gently while stirring until the sugar has melted.

Let the syrup simmer at low heat until it thickens. Add the orange peels and cook at low heat for approximately 15 minutes or until the strips caramelize. Take the pan off the heat and leave the orange strips to cool but not set in the pan. Gently remove the orange peel strips from the pan and let them drain on a tray or cookie sheet covered with parchment paper. Sprinkle sugar over the strips and store them in the freezer.

TIPS AND TRICKS

Feel free to save some of the orange syrup and use it to drizzle over soft cakes, ice cream, or other desserts.

It's also nice to dip candied orange peel in melted chocolate (see page 16). Place the chocolate dipped shells on a baking sheet and allow to solidify in the refrigerator.

SMASHED "ICE CHOCOLATE"

with candied ginger

MAKES ABOUT 25 PIECES

INGREDIENTS
4–5 PIECES CANDIED GINGER
4.5 OZ DARK CHOCOLATE (55–70%)
4.5 OZ MILK CHOCOLATE
7 OZ SOLID COCONUT OIL
3 TSP GOLDEN SYRUP

Chop the ginger, place it in a bowl, and cover with plastic wrap. Chop the chocolate. In a saucepan, melt the coconut oil. Take the pan off the heat and add the chocolate and let it melt while stirring. Add the syrup. Turn out the chocolate mixture onto a small cookie sheet or tray covered with parchment paper. Sprinkle the chopped candied ginger over the chocolate.

Let set in the fridge for 2 to 3 hours. Transfer the chocolate onto a cutting board. Cut or break it into about 25 pieces and store in a cool place before serving.

TIPS AND TRICKS
Ginger is a lovely spice for the holidays. To add more flavor, you can sprinkle the chocolate with powdered ginger.

CHOCOLATE AND CARAMEL CANDY APPLES

with roasted salted almonds

MAKES 8 APPLES

INGREDIENTS

8 UNPAINTED WOODEN DOWELS / FLORAL PICKS / BAMBOO SKEWERS
8 APPLES
3.5 OZ SALTED ROASTED ALMONDS
3.5 OZ DARK CHOCOLATE (55–70%)
5.25 OZ (1⅓ STICKS) BUTTER
½ CUP + 1 TBSP GRANULATED SUGAR
¾ CUPS GOLDEN SYRUP, DIVIDED
FOOD / CANDY THERMOMETER

Rinse and dry the apples carefully. Let them cool in the fridge for about 1 hour. Chop the nuts and place them on a deep plate. Chop the chocolate. In a saucepan, combine the butter, sugar, and ½ cup of the syrup. Heat the mixture while stirring until the sugar has melted. Simmer until the temperature reaches 284°F (140°C), or until the mixture starts to caramelize and turns light brown (approximately 10 minutes). Take the pan off the heat and mix in the chocolate and the remainder of the syrup and stir until the mixture is smooth.

Transfer the chocolate caramel into a high narrow dish with enough room for an apple. Place a skewer/floral stick into the middle of each apple and dip them first into the chocolate caramel, and then roll them in the chopped nuts. Place the finished apples to cool on a cookie sheet or tray covered with parchment paper.

TIPS AND TRICKS

Be careful when you work with the caramel mixture because it gets very hot. If you'd like to involve children when you're making the candy apples, make sure that you keep a watchful eye on them, or perhaps have them make the chocolate-dipped apples instead (see page 107).

SNOW-WHITE ROCKY ROAD

MAKES 15 SLICES

INGREDIENTS
3.5 OZ MARSHMALLOWS (PINK AND WHITE)
1 CUP PISTACHIO NUTS
18 OZ WHITE CHOCOLATE
1 CUP DRIED CRANBERRIES OR DRIED CHERRIES

Cut the marshmallows into small pieces. Chop the nuts. Melt the chocolate (see page 16) and let it cool but not set. Layer the chocolate, marshmallows, nuts, and cranberries in a loaf pan (approximately 3 x 8 inches) covered with parchment paper cut to size. Let cool before placing the pan in the fridge to set. Cut into slices to serve.

TIPS AND TRICKS
Rocky Road is always a favorite on the dessert table for the holidays. This white chocolate variation will be popular with all ages. If you prefer, you can use pastel-colored marshmallows (pale yellow, mint green, and pale blue). Serve the Rocky Road sliced in slices or cut into cubes.

SOFT LICORICE FUDGE "KOLA" CARAMELS

MAKES 16 PIECES

INGREDIENTS

3.5 OZ DARK CHOCOLATE (55–70%)
2 TBSP COCOA POWDER
1 TSP LICORICE POWDER
1 STICK / 3.5 OZ BUTTER
¾ CUP + 1 TSP HEAVY CREAM
¾ CUP + 1 TSP MUSCOVADO BROWN
SUGAR (LIGHT OR DARK)
¾ CUP + 1 TSP LIQUID GLUCOSE
FLAKY SEA SALT
FOOD / CANDY THERMOMETER

Chop the chocolate and mix with the cocoa and licorice powder. Let the butter rest at room temperature for about 20 minutes. In a heavy saucepan, combine cream, muscovado sugar, and glucose. Cook at medium heat while stirring until the mixture measures 241°F (116°C) on your thermometer.

Take the pan off the heat, add the licorice mixture, and beat with an electric mixer. Add the soft butter in stages. Pour the "Kola" mixture onto a tray (about 3 x 8 inches), which is covered with parchment paper. Leave to cool and set. Cut the "Kola" into pieces and sprinkle it with the flaky sea salt. Store in a cool place.

FRUIT JELLY BITES

MAKES 40 PIECES

INGREDIENTS

¾ CUP + 1 TSP APPLE JUICE CONCENTRATE
¾ CUP + 1 TSP WATER
6 FL OZ LIQUID PECTIN
2 CUPS + 1 TBSP SUGAR, DIVIDED

GARNISH:
ABOUT ¾ CUP SUGAR

Boil the juice and water in a pot. Add the liquid pectin and stir in with 2 tablespoons of the sugar and boil for 5 minutes. Add the rest of the sugar and boil while stirring until all the sugar has de-solved. Boil at a high temperature until the mixture is a bit sticky, to 230°F (110°C) on a food/candy thermometer.

Pour the mix into a heat-resistant form, about 6 x 10 inches, and let harden overnight. Cut into pieces. Sift half of the sugar for garnish and overturn the jelly bites on a piece of baking paper. Carefully mix with the rest of the sugar.

TIPS AND TRICKS
Store the Fruit Jelly Bites in layers in a tin with each layer separated by parchment paper. To make the color orange, mix yellow and red food coloring.

RECIPE LIST

SWEDISH CHRISTMAS TREATS
is as nice to give as a gift as it is to keep for yourself. The recipes in the book are easy to make, delicious, and wonderfully festive!

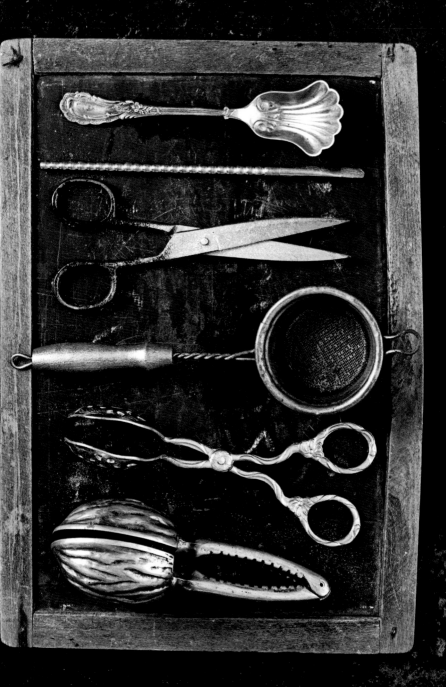

CONVERSION CHART
(DL TO US CUPS)

DL	US Cups
½	¼
⅔	⅓
¾	⅓
1	⅓ + 1 TBSP
1¼	½
1⅓	½
1½	½ + 1 TBSP
1¾	¾
2	¾ + 1 TSP
2¼	1
2⅓	1
2½	1 + 1 TSP
2¾	1¼
3	1¼
3½	1½
4	1⅔
4½	2
5	2 + 1 TBSP